D1810462

101 Coolest Things to Do in Costa Rica

Introduction

So you're going to Costa Rica, huh? You lucky lucky
thing! You are sure in for a treat because Costa Rica is
truly one of the most magical countries on this planet.

This guide will take you on a journey from the capital
city, San Jose, to attractions in the gills such as wildlife
parks and coffee plantations, right through to quaint
beach towns where you can go snorkelling in the ocean
or just work on your tan.

In this guide, we'll be giving you the low down on:
- the very best things to shove in your pie hole, from
typical Costa Rican bar snacks through to the best
places to purchase Costa Rican coffee
- the best shopping so that you can take a little piece of
Costa Rica home with you, whether that's in the form
of an indigenous mask or a piece of original
photography
- incredible festivals, whether you would like to rock
out to Latin American bands in a tidal island or you'd

like to celebrate an indigenous festival in the hills of the countryside.

- the coolest historical and cultural sights that you simply cannot afford to miss from mysterious spheres found in the jungle through to stunning churches

- the best places to have a few cocktails and party with the local people

- and tonnes more coolness besides!

Let's not waste any more time – here are the 101 coolest things not to miss in Costa Rica!

1. Say Hi to Leatherback Sea Turtles in Las Baulas National Marine Park

Animal lovers need to get themselves to Costa Rica pronto. This country is a veritable haven for all kinds of animal life, and many species that are rarely found. One such species is the leatherback sea turtle, which is the largest turtle on the face of the earth, and the fourth heaviest reptile. On a trip to Las Baulas National Marine Park, it's possible to see these breath taking creatures in person. A turtle conservation tour will take you to see the turtles, and you can also learn about the conservation efforts of the park.

(Guanacaste Province; www.leatherback.org/get-involved/join-us/las-baulas-national-park/visit-las-baulas)

2. Have a Birdwatching Adventure in Bosque Nuboso Monteverde

Yes, there are tonnes of incredible animals all over Costa Rica, and if you are an animal lover, it's imperative that you don't forget to look to the skies, because the amount of bird life in this country is second to none. Bosque Nuboso Monteverde is a cloud forest reserve, and it is the best place in the whole country for birdwatching. Bring your binoculars and you might see swallow tailed kites, piratic flycatchers, and many other exotic species besides.

(Carretera a Reserva de Monteverde, Provincia de Puntarenas, Monte Verde; www.cloudforestmonteverde.com/bosque-nuboso.html)

3. Dare to Discover Fiestas de Los Diablitos

If you really want to get to grips with Costa Rica, you have to take the time to learn about its indigenous culture, and we think there's no more exciting way of doing this than by exploring the Fiestas de los Diablitos, which translates as the festivals of the little devils. This festival takes place in the villages of Boruca and Rey Curre where the Brunka tribe lives. Men from the villages dress up as bulls and devils and dance around fires, and tourists are very welcome to visit and watch.

4. Tuck Into a Bowl of Chifrijo

Every country in the world has its own variant on bar food and bar snacks, and Costa Rica is no different. If you want something savoury to consume while sinking a cold beer at a beach bar, we can't recommend a heaped bowl of chifrijo highly enough. Chifrijo is essentially the layering of rice, beans, some kind of meat, and chimichurri, which is a tangy tomato salad. The meat is usually fried pork meat or pork skins. It's the best thing for a late night snack.

5. Pay a Visit to the Artsy Town of Sarchi

If you are an arts lover through and through, you absolutely cannot miss the quaint arts town of Sarchi, which is located in the hilly Alajuela region of the country. Take a stroll around this town and you will be bowled away by the amount of colour that you take in from the objects in the shops and stalls all over the streets. Here, you can shop for all kinds of handicrafts, so whether you want to take home some beautiful earrings, stunning textile work, or some of the masks typical of the country, you certainly won't leave empty handed.

6. Visit an Organic Chocolate Farm, La Iguana Chocolate

If you are a chocolate fan, and who isn't, you are in the right place, because Costa Rica produces some of the finest cacao in the world. If you want to truly get to the roots of chocolate in Costa Rica, it can be a great idea to visit the La Iguana Chocolate organic chocolate farm. The staff will be very happy to take you on a chocolate tour through the rainforest, and there are even rooms at the farm, so if you want to have a truly local experience, you can stick around for a while.

(La Iguana Chocolate Mastatal, Puriscal; www.laiguanachocolate.com)

7. Take in a Show at the Teatro Nacional

Costa Rica might be best known for its landscapes and wildlife, but what about when evening rolls around and you want to be entertained? Well, that is when you book yourself a seat at the stunning Teatro Nacional in

San Jose, the most important theatre in the country. In fact, not only the most important theatre, as it's often considered to be the most important historic building in the capital too. Do keep your eyes on the programme of events because the National Symphonic Orchestra often performs here.

(Av Central, Provincia de San José, San José, 5015-1000; www.teatronacional.go.cr)

8. Stay in a Treehouse in the Dense Jungle

When you think of Costa Rica, you probably think of jungle and rainforest. While it can be great to explore this aspect of the country by taking hikes in nature, how much cooler would it be if you could actually spend the night in the jungle? Well, it turns out that you can. Nature Observatorio is a luxury treehouse that sits deep in the jungle, far away from any roads. It has all the mod-cons of modern luxury, but you'll be in the jungle with only the sounds of nature around you.

(Calle El Arbol 2, Provincia de Limón, Manzanillo; www.natureobservatorio.com)

9. Try Your Hand at Sport Fishing Off the Coast of Quepos

Costa Rica has coastline on both sides, and this means that there is ample opportunity for some awesome activities in the water, such as sport fishing. One of our favourite places for this is Quepos, where you'll find a handful of companies who specialise in just this. Fisherman will take you out on their boats for the whole day, and show you the ropes so that you can reel in some humungous fish. Fish that live in these waters include blue marlin, yellow fin, snapper, and plenty more besides

10. Ride the Country's First Zip Line in Monteverde

If you fancy yourself as something of a thrill seeker, you are in luck, because there are plenty of opportunities to have hair raising and heart racing adventures in the wild of Costa Rica. There are now countless canopy tours in the country, but the original and still the best is in Monteverde. In fact, there is a zip line there that extends for a whole kilometre. It's certainly not for the faint hearted, but if you are feeling brave, it is a wonderful and unique way of exploring the jungle canopy.

11. Dance With Total Abandon at Envision Festival

When you think of places around the world where you can party hard at summer festivals, Costa Rica is unlikely to be at the top of your list. With that said, there is certainly a festival culture within the country, and one of the most fun of them all has to be Envision Festival, which takes place on Uvita island, a tidal island in the Pacific coast. Many Latin artists are invited to perform at the event, so you can splash around in the waves by day and dance under the stars at night.
(http://envisionfestival.com)

12. Swim in a Waterfall Pool at Llanos de Cortes

As a country known for its outdoor beauty, you won't have a hard time finding cascading waterfalls in Costa Rica, but in our opinion the most beautiful of them all has to be Llanos de Cortes. This waterfall is twelve metres and high and fifteen metres wide, and the sound of the pounding water is almost deafening. The waterfalls drop into a pool with a sandy beach, which is perfect for swimming and relaxing. And since there are no amenities, you will really feel as though you have been dropped into the middle of nature.

13. Try Your Hand at Surfing on Playa Grande

Costa Rica has no shortage of stunning beaches. But there's only so much topping up of your tan you can do before you start to get bored. Luckily, there are tonnes of activities that will keep you from being bored right out there on the waves. If you've never tried surfing before, this is the time. One of the best beaches for surf in the country is Playa Grande, a beach on the Pacific coast. There are numerous surf schools here that can teach you everything you need to ride those waves right from the basics.

14. Donate Some Time With Proyecto Montezuma

When you go on holiday, it's the time to relax and get away from it all. But it can also be a time when you want to try new things and gain some perspective on your life. And one of the best things for this is to offer your time as a volunteer. There are many volunteer projects around Costa Rica, and Proyecto Montezuma is one of our favourites. You can donate your time teaching English to kids and adults, and you can stay at the facility on the beach too.

(www.proyectomontezuma.org)

15. Enjoy a Spicy Bowl of Rondon on the Beach

If you have a taste for spicy food, you need to become acquainted with rondon sooner rather than later. This dish actually originates from Jamaica, which is why you will only really see it on the Caribbean coast of the country. Essentially, this is a spicy broth of coconut milk and various chillies and spices that is cooked with whatever fish can be caught that day from the sea. The result is something exotic, totally delicious, and full of the fresh flavours of the ocean.

16. Visit Guatil Village for Chorotega Pottery

To really understand a country, you have to get to grips with its handicrafts, and one of the most beautiful things that you can find in Costa Rica is the Chorotega Pottery. In a small village called Guatil, families are dedicated to making this pottery, and having been doing so for generations. Clay from the nearby mountains is mixed with iguana sand, and then the pottery is thrown by hand, and glazed with natural minerals.

17. Take a Boat Ride in Cano Negro Nature Reserve

If you have hiked just about as many kilometres as you can possibly muster, you'll be glad to know that there are some other, less tiring, ways of exploring the beautiful landscapes of Costa Rica. This wildlife reserve sits on the border of Nicaragua, and because the reserve is so wet, it can only be explored by boat. Your four hour boat tour of the park will take you on a floating journey through the rainforest, marshlands, and pastures.

18. Discover Costa Rica's Coffee Plantations at Finca Rosa Blanca

Costa Rica is famous for its delicious coffee that gets exported to different countries all over the world. If you want to get to grips with this coffee culture, the best thing to do is to visit a coffee plantation. There's more than a few of these strewn around the country, but we particularly like Finca Rosa Blanca, which is a coffee plantation resort where you can actually stay and take in the culture. And, of course, it's a wonderful place to buy some coffee beans to take home.

(Barrio Jesús de Santa Bárbara de Heredia, Hotel Finca Rosa Blanca, Heredia; www.fincarosablanca.com/en)

19. Party Til the Early Hours at Club Vertigo

While you probably haven't ventured all the way to Costa Rica just to go to nightclubs, this is not to say that there is not a thriving party scene in the country's capital, and if you love to party the night away, you are sure to feel at home at Club Vertigo. Without a doubt, one of Costa Rica's premier nightclubs, here you'll find two huge rooms and a state of the art sound system. It's an awesome place to let loose and party with the locals.

(http://vertigocr.com)

20. Celebrate the Corn Fiesta in Upala

The Upala region of Costa Rica is very agricultural and the crop of choice there is corn. To celebrate the beautiful corn that comes from the area, each year there is a corn festival called Fiestas del Maiz. This event is celebrated on every October 13th and you can expect lots of fun stuff. There will be a parade through the streets with outfits made entirely out of corn, and the peak of the festival is the crowning of the Corn Queen. Of course, there's always lots of corn to eat too.

21. Luxuriate in the Black Sands of Playa Negra

Costa Rica has more of its fair share of beautiful beaches, and some of these are really unique. One of our favourites is called Playa Negra, which can be found on the Pacific coast, just south of Tamarindo. The really incredible thing about this beach is that the sand is perfectly black, making for some really special holiday photographs. It's also a wonderful place for surfing, so if you fancy hitting the waves, you'll be in good company.

22. Find Something to Eat at Samara Farmers' Market

Samara is an adorable costal town in the Guanacaste region. As well as hosting a beach with beautifully white sand, one of the highlights of life in peaceful Samara is the weekly farmers' market you can find there. The market supports local organic farmers, and as well as being able to find tasty fruits and veggies, you can find more artisanal items such as freshly baked breads, hummus, bagels, and there's even a massage stall if you really want to unwind.

23. Immerse Yourself in Tropical Fruits at Finca La Isla

If you love nothing more than to completely immerse yourself in incredible nature, you have definitely come to the right country. Yes, the national parks are fabulous, but if you are looking for something on a smaller scale, we can totally recommend Finca de Isla. This farm and botanical garden is the place to immerse yourself in a world of exotic plants and many tropical fruits. Organic peppers, cacao, and 150 species of tropical fruits are grown here.

24. Sip on a Refreshing Glass of Agua de Sapo

When we are desperate for a way to cool down in the midday sun of a Costa Rica beach town and there is no air conditioning in sight, we always grab an Agua de Sapo, the most refreshing drink in the country. This is a drink that is made from tapa de dulce, which is basically unrefined sugar, limes, and ginger. The result is something fresh and cooling and that is perfect for a lazy afternoon of topping up your tan on the beach.

25. Visit the Studio of Folk Painter, Fran Vazquez

Costa Rica might be a country that is more famous for its landscapes, beaches, and outdoor adventures, but if you are an artsy type of person, we don't think that Costa Rica will disappoint you. In an isolated part of the country on a road to Bribri, you can find the working studio of local folk painter, Fran Vazquez. The painter is entirely self taught, and his beautiful folk landscapes are popular right throughout the country. One of his paintings might just be the perfect thing to take home with you.

26. Peek into a Volcano's Crater at Parque Nacional Volcan Poas

The National Park of Volcan Poas provides one of the most unique landscapes in all of Costa Rica. This park is home to an active volcano that has a history of eruptions that dates back a staggering 11 million years, with its last major eruption in 1910. As you walk around the park, you can actually see the cavernous craters of the volcano, and sometimes you might see sulphurous emissions coming from the landscape as well.

27. Chow Down at the International Food Fair in San Jose

While there are some tasty dishes to be found around Costa Rica, most people don't travel to this central American country just for the food. But if you are a foodie through to your bones, the good news is that an International Food Fair is hosted every March in a San Jose suburb called Coronado. This fair celebrates the food not just from Costa Rica, but from over 30 countries around the world, so there is sure to be something that suits even the fussiest of eaters.

28. Ease Your Muscles in the Hot Springs of Rio Perdido

If you want to explore the incredible beauty of Costa Rica's landscapes, but you don't want to compromise on luxury, we wholeheartedly recommend a stay at Rio

Perdido. This luxury resort is set within the middle of a 600 acre reserve. In the day times you can go on adventurous hikes throughout the park, and in the evening you can return and enjoy a relaxing dip in the resorts very own thermal pools. Sounds good to us.

29. Try the Costa Rican Blood Sausage, Morcilla

Okay, morcilla isn't exactly something that comes directly from Costa Rica as it is popular in many Latin American countries, but that doesn't stop it from being both delicious and available, so make sure that you tuck into some. Morcilla is essentially the Latin version of a blood sausage. In Costa Rica, the pig's blood is typically combined with sweet potato and onions, creating a sweeter sausage than in other parts of the world.

30. Brush Up Your Spanish Skills

Costa Rica is, of course, a Spanish speaking country, and knowing some Spanish will help you every day to have the very best trip possible, and connect to the local people in a much deeper way. Fortunately, there are tonnes of Spanish schools all over the country so that you can get to grips with Spanish basics before embarking on your travels. We advise enrolling in a one week course (at least), right at the beginning of your trip. We particularly like the Tamarindo Spanish School where you can stay with local families.

(www.tamarindospanishschool.org)

31. Take an Iguana Conservation Tour

Costa Rica is a country that is bursting full with incredible wildlife, but sadly, some of the wildlife is in danger, and numbers of certain species are dwindling. The green iguana is one such species, and you can learn more about the animal, its life in Costa Rica, and how the Iguana Verde company are helping to repopulate the species in the wild on an Iguana Conservation Tour. During the tour, you'll have the opportunity to learn lots more about this unique animal and visit the iguana enclosure where you can actually interact with the reptiles.

32. Find a Little Piece of Paradise at Playa Cocles

If you are a beach bum through and through and your idea of the perfect break is hopping from sandy beach to sandy beach, you need to pay a visit to Playa Cocles on the Atlantic south coast before leaving Costa Rica. Playa Cocles is very much a local village. It only has two stores! This means that if you really want to get away from it all and find a slice of paradise unlike anywhere else in the world, Playa Cocles is the destination for you.

33. Visit a Fairtrade Gallery in San Jose, Galeria Namu

To feel the contemporary creative energy of any country, you need to explore the capital city, and the same can be said of Costa Rica where there are many thriving independent galleries and creative enterprises in San Jose. One of our favourites is Galeria Nemu.

The gallery brings together creative works from all over the country, and it's a place to lay your hands on something truly special, whether that happens to be a Guaymi doll, a Boruca mask, or a beautifully hand crafted reed mat.

(Av. 7 between Calles 5 and 7, San Jose; http://galerianamu.com)

34. Look Out for Harpy Eagles in Parque Nacional La Amistad

There are very few people who ever have the opportunity to see the incredible Harpy Eagle out in the wild. This is one of the heaviest and most distinctive looking birds of prey on the planet, and if you want to try and look for one, the La Amistad National Park in the south of the country is the place to be. The park is relatively unexplored because of the difficulty of its terrain, but if you are something of an adventurer, it could be just what you are looking for.

35. Cool Down With a Refreshing Batido

To say that Costa Rica is a warm country is something of an understatement, and when you are by the beach it can be staggeringly hot. The heat can be exhausting, and the best way to cool down is with a refreshing batido. This, essentially, is the Costa Rican version of a smoothie. This blended up fruit and ice drinks are all natural, and you are sure to find a flavour that you love. For something a little but different, we love the tanginess of a sour guava batido. Yum!

36. Relax in the La Paz Waterfall Gardens

When you find yourself in the Costa Rican capital, San Jose, with a desire to get away from the hustle and bustle, there is nothing that beats a day trip to the La Paz Waterfall Gardens, which are only an hour outside of the city. These gardens, which can be found on the slopes of the Poas volcano, contain the largest butterfly observatory in the whole world, five stunning waterfalls, hiking trails, a serpentarium, and hummingbird gardens.

(126, Alajuela Province;

www.waterfallgardens.com/la_paz_waterfall_gardens.php)

37. Explore the Largest Archaeological Site in the Country

While it's true that Costa Rica doesn't have the same scale of archaeological sites as some other places in Latin America, if you are a history buff, there are still some treasures to be found around the country, and Guayabo is the jewel in that crown. This 232 hectare monument was only discovered in the 1960s, and much of it is still to be explored. The city site dates way back to 1000 BC, and interesting pottery and gold artefacts have been found on digs here.

(Cartago Province, Turrialba)

38. Eat a Refreshing Plate of Ceviche Tico

When you think of ceviche, fresh fish cooked in lime juice, Peru is probably the first country that comes to mind, but Costa Rica also has its own version of ceviche, and we think that it's pretty darn delicious. To be honest, ceviche is not a one size fits all kind of dish, and it will change depending on the part of the coast where you happen to be. But that's the real beauty of it. Wherever you are, the fish will be fresh and is going to taste superb.

39. Shop for Souvenirs at Kiosko SJO

If you are down to your last few days in Costa Rica and you still need to do your souvenir shopping, don't fly into a panic and buy the rubbish that is sold in the tourist shops, but head to Kiosko SJO in San Jose instead. The focus in this quaint shop is on sustainable design by Latin American artisans, and once inside, you can find all manner of goodies. Highlights include leather boots and bags made by hand, artisanal chocolate bars, handmade jewellery, and original photography.

40. Go Horseback Riding Along Drake Bay

The Osa peninsula of Costa Rica is one of the less explored parts of the country, and in our opinion, that's all the more reason to go exploring. Drake Bay is a small bay on the north of the peninsula, and it was given its name because Francis drake was said to have used the port in the 16th century. This bay is really beautiful for hiking and for snorkelling, but we think if you really want to connect with nature in a unique way, you can't beat a horseback ride along the bay in the Costa Rican sunshine.

41. Indulge With a Few Guaro Sours

A holiday in Costa Rica is totally the time to be indulgent, and what could be more indulgent than knocking back a few cocktails, whether it's on a lazy beach day or at a fancy bar in San Jose? One of our favourite concoctions to be found in Costa Rica is the Guaro Sour. The most important ingredient here is guaro, which is alcohol made from the sugar cane, and this is mixed up with fresh lime, a sprig of mint, and club soda. Super refreshing.

42. Have a Day of Learning at the Pre-Columbian Gold Museum

While Costa Rica isn't so much of a country for great museums, there certainly are some wonderful museums there, and the pre-Columbian Gold Museum has to be one of the best of them all. Located in San Jose, this museum has a substantial collection of more than 1600 artefacts of pre-Columbian gold, some of which dates all the way back to the year 500 AD. Inside, you'll find amulets, earrings, figurines, and even erotic statuettes. *(Calle 5, Provincia de San José)*

43. Discover the Country's Cacao Culture on the Cacao Trails

If you are something of a chocoholic, it's absolutely necessary that you become acquainted with Cacao Trails. These botanical gardens and chocolate museum combined can be found a little inland from the south Caribbean coast of the country. Inside the chocolate museum, you will actually find a working chocolate factory so that you can really get to grips with how chocolate is made there. And afterwards, you are welcome to take it easy by walking around the lush gardens.

(Limón Province; www.cacaotrails.com)

44. Be Wowed by the Beautiful Coronado Church

Costa Rica is a country that tourists tend to visit more for its natural beauty than for its architecture, but if you are a fan of religious architecture, we highly recommend a trip to the Coronado Church in the city of Coronado, which lies just outside of the capital, San Jose. This church was built in a neo-gothic style in 1935 with a metal framework, and beautifully elaborate stained glass windows.

45. Find Something Special at Biesanz Woodworks

Before you leave Costa Rica, you will no doubt want to take back some really special artefacts that will always remind you of this stunning country, and if you are interested in hand crafted artisan goods, we cannot recommend Biesanz Woodworks in the hills of Bello Horizante highly enough. Acclaimed woodworker, Barry Biesanz uses pre-Columbian techniques and creates all his bowls and other decorative receptacles by hand. These means they aren't cheap, but the love that goes into every object is evident.

(33 Calle 110/Calle El Pedrero, Escazu; www.biesanz.com)

46. Visit a Farmer's Market in San Jose

One of the best ways to have a local experience in any country is to visit a local market, and Costa Rica is absolutely no different. If you are in San Jose on a Saturday morning and at a loss as to what to do, we can totally recommend a trip to the Feria Verde de Aranjuez, a weekly farmer's market, which is particularly popular with foodies from around the capital. You'll find freshly baked cakes, artisanal coffee, yummy chocolate bars, and loads more to boot.

(Calle 19, San José; www.feriaverde.org)

47. Take in a Football Match at the National Stadium

Costa Rica is a national full of football lovers, and if you are the sporty type, one of the highlights of your trip will surely be taking in a football match in the epic National Stadium in San Jose. This stadium is hugely impressive, and can fit a staggering 35,000 people inside. There is nothing quite like the sound of 35,000 people cheering on the national team, and it must be experienced if you are a sports fan. Keep your eyes on their timetable of matches.

(Av. de Las Américas, San José)

48. Kayak Through the Mangroves of Corcovado

Corcovado National Park is one of the most isolated and special areas of natural beauty in Costa Rica, not least because it contains the largest area of mangrove anywhere in Central America. Fortunately, there are mangrove forest tours that you can take, and you will be shown around the whole mangrove in the only way possible – by boat. This part of the park is home to boa constrictors, crocodiles, tree frogs, iguanas, and river turtles.

(www.corcovadoguide.com)

49. Tuck into Tamales at Christmas Time

Christmas time is definitely the time of year when it's okay to indulge and take in a few more calories than you normally would, and this applies if you are in Costa Rica for the Christmas period as well. One of the traditional things to eat in the run up to Christmas in Costa Rica is tamales. Tamales in Costa Rica are typically filled with juicy pork meat and sweet peppers, and then wrapped to steam in banana leaves.

50. Party Thought the Night at Jaco

Jaco is one of those places that you either love or you hate, and it really divides travellers who pay a visit. This tiny little beach village is a party spot where hippies and backpackers party right throughout the night. There is definitely a devil may care attitude here, and if you want a tranquil beach break this might not be the place for you. But if you want to party and meet other travellers, we're sure that you will feel perfectly at home.

51. Watch a Show at Teatro Melico Salazar

Costa Rica is a nature over culture kind of country, but this is not to say that you can't find some incredible cultural events across the country, and particularly in San Jose. One of the best destinations for a cultural night on the town has to be the Teatro Melico Salazar, a theatre that opened in the centre of San Jose in the 1920s. To this day, the theatre maintains a full schedule of concerts, recitals, and plays, so if you want a reason to get dressed up be sure to keep up to date with their programme of events.

(Calle Central Alfredo Volio, Provincia de San José; www.teatromelico.go.cr/portal)

52. Try to Find the Jaguars in Corcovado National Park

With so much dense jungle and forest in Costa Rica, you can, of course, find jungle animals, including the stunning jaguar. If you want to see jaguars for yourself, the best place to take a hike is in the Corcovado National Park. Jaguars are the third largest cats in the world, and a true sight to behold, but if you do happen to see one of these majestic cats, you will be very lucky, but it's normally only one or two people that manage to spot a jaguar in the tourist season. But trying never hurt anyone.

53. Indulge a Sweet Tooth with a Slice of Tres Leches Cake

If you have a sweet tooth, you might be disappointed to know that Costa Rica doesn't have the strongest of baking cultures. With that said, a Costa Rican cake that we'd happily tuck into on any given day is the Tres

Leches Cakes. This cake is not for the faint hearted because it involves a delicious buttery sponge being soaked in three different types of milk: evaporated milk, condensed milk, and heavy cream. But why not indulge?

54. Go Fishing on Lake Arenal

If your idea of the perfect getaway is to sit by the edge of a lake with a fishing rod and wait for a great catch, you are definitely in for a treat in Costa Rica, because there are quite a few fishing destinations, and Lake Arenal is certainly one of the most popular of them all. Lake Arenal has an area of 85 square kilometres, which makes it the largest lake in the country, and means that it's full of fish. Some of the fish you might catch in the lake include machaca and rainbow bass.

55. Join in With the Limon Carnival Celebrations

If you want to get to grips with the rich Afro-Caribbean culture of Costa Rica, there is truly nothing better than heading to Limon during October for the exciting carnival celebrations that take place every year. The carnival is a celebration of the arrival of Christopher Columbus to Costa Rica's coast in the 16th century, and it's a wild party. You can expect lots of calypso music on the streets, colourful costumes, dancing until the early hours, and lots of yummy food like coconut rice and jerk chicken.

56. Have a History Lesson at the National Museum of Costa Rica

While it's true that Costa Rica is much more of a place for nature lovers rather than culture vultures, there are definitely some museums that will keep fans of history and culture happy. The National Museum of Costa Rica, located in the capital city, is probably the most celebrated of them all. As you walk through the aisles of the museum you'll be taken on a journey through the country's history, with pre-hispanic artefacts, items from the civil war, and much more besides.

(Cuesta de Moras, Provincia de San José)

57. Trek the Montezuma Waterfalls

There is nothing quite as relaxing as taking a hike in nature to a flowing waterfall, and then taking a dip in its waters. Fortunately, there's more than a few options for serious waterfall lovers visiting Costa Rica, and the Montezuma Waterfalls are some of the best loved falls in the country. The Montezuma Falls are actually a set of three different cascades, and the good news is that all the falls have pools that are safe for swimming. And the top waterfall has a fun rope swing too.

58. Discover the Country's Mysterious Stone Spheres

One of the greatest mysteries of Costa Rica, is the country's stone spheres. Back in the 1930s, over 300 perfectly round and smooth stone spheres were found deep in the country's jungle, some a few inches in diameter, while some extended more than seven feet across. It is now possible for visitors to journey to these spheres in the middle of the countryside in a site specific museum. Experts believe that they date way back to the year 600, and that they were made by indigenous people.

59. Enjoy the Hot Springs of Piscinas de los Pobres

Pisicina de los Pobres, which can be translated as the pools of the poor, is the place where the local people come to relax and unwind. This place is situated eight miles from La Fortuna, and pretty much the only way to get there is to hike. Once you get there, it will so be worth the effort. You will find that two thermal rivers converge to a create a thermal pool where you can soak your tired muscles in the quietude of nature.

60. Immerse Yourself in Silence at Playa Zancudo

If your idea of the perfect trip away is to get away from it all, we are certain that you'll fall head over hills for the perfectly tranquil coastal village of Zancudo on the Pacific coast of the country. The population here is just 450, so you can bet your bottom dollar that you are hardly going to see any tourists, and maybe not even any locals. If you want a quiet beach to yourself and all the time and space in the world to centre yourself, Playa Zancudo should be at the very top of your hit list.

61. Walk Through the Aisles of Mercado Central in San Jose

To get to grips with any city, you have to visit its markets. The markets are the lifeblood of a city, where people go to buy their food and negotiate on prices. In San Jose, the main market is definitely Mercado Central. While Costa Rica has a reputation as not being one of the cheapest places in Central America, everything in this market is cheap as chips. You'll be able to find coffee beans, cacao, trinkets, and many other things. It's well worth spending a couple of hours perusing the aisles.

(Av. Central, San José)

62. Get Close to Jungle Animals at the Jaguar Rescue Centre

While there are jaguars in the wild in Costa Rica, it is extremely rare that any tourist will have the opportunity to see them, but if you visit the Jaguar Rescue Centre, a very well run wildlife rescue facility, you are a certain to see a jaguar up close. They also have many other wild animals, such as sloths, monkeys, and raptors. If you want a truly one of a kind experience, the rescue centre also accepts volunteers for a minimum of three weeks.

(Limón Province, Punta Cocles; www.jaguarrescue.foundation)

63. Party Like a Cowboy at Fiestas Palmares

If you are lucky enough to be visiting Costa Rica during the month of January, you will have the opportunity to join in with the festivities of one of the most important celebrations of the year: Fiestas Palmares. It is said that this is the festival where you can party like a cowboy, but truly there is something for everybody. It is hosted in the small town of Palmares, and each year you can find live music concerts, bullfighting, stand-comedy, plenty of eating and drinking, and lots of other merrymakers out to have a great time.

64. Hike Along the Rio Celeste

The Rio Celeste is possibly the most beautiful of all the rivers in Costa Rica, with incredible deep blue water, and this makes it a superb hiking destination for tourists in the country. The most popular hike along the river is to the Rio Celeste waterfall, which is a relatively tricky hike with some hilly parts. Once you arrive, however, you will be rewarded by a thundering waterfall and the opportunity to cool down and take a dip.

65. Get Cultural at the CENAC Summer Festival

CENAC, which is the Ministry of Youth and Culture for Costa Rica, hosts its very own festival every February in the downtown area of San Jose. For culture vultures, this is one of the very best events of the year with a mix of live concerts, dance shows, storytelling, drama shows, and movie screenings. It's a great way of exploring the talents of local people in Costa Rica while being entertained.

66. Tuck Into Yummy Cacoa Fresco

Cacao is an extremely important part of Costa Rica's agriculture, and while you might just be used to consuming chocolate in a chocolate bar and once in a while as a hot chocolate, the uses for cacao are far more wide reaching in Costa Rica. In fact, the local people like to eat the tender flesh of the pods that surrounds the cacao beans, and this is called cacao fresco. The fruit is sweet and tangy, and you might not even believe that it comes from the cacao plant.

67. Stay With Local People by Using Couchsurfing

There are countless things for tourists to see and do on a trip to Costa Rica, but if you really want to get off the beaten path and experience Costa Rica like the locals do, you need to live like one of the locals. Couchsurfing.com is a website that can help with this. Locals with a spare couch or a spare bed advertise their space and let you stay for free. Of course, this is great for those on a budget, but the true value comes from the cultural exchange that you'll experience.

(www.couchsurfing.com)

68. Learn About Sloths at the Sloth Sanctuary of Costa Rica

Is there any animal on this planet cuter than the sloth? Well, you can see your fair share of this cute as pie animal at the Sloth Sanctuary of Costa Rica, which is the most important sloth sanctuary in the whole world. A visit to the sanctuary will give you the opportunity to learn more about these fascinating cuties, and how the people in the park look after them. We guarantee that you'll be desperate for a pet sloth by the time you leave. *(36, Limón Province; www.slothsanctuary.com)*

69. Enjoy the Fun of San Jose Carnival

The people of Costa Rica certainly do like to celebrate and have a good time, and you will find this out for yourself if you visit San Jose on December 27th, which is the date of the annual San Jose carnival. As with any carnival worth its salt, the centre of the festivities is a huge parade with colourful floats that make their way down the streets of the city's downtown area. This is a very inclusive event, and everybody is welcome to join in and have some fun.

70. Learn How to Cook Costa Rican Goodies

One of the great pleasures of visiting a foreign country is sampling all of the yummy food that it has to offer. But how much more impressive would it be if you could actually cook up some of that Costa Rican grub when you return to your home country? Pretty darn impressive, and that's why it's a great idea to take at least one cooking class, and we are particularly fond of the classes at Guayabo Lodge in Santa Cruz. They have one off cooking classes, but also cooking school immersion that lasts for 4 days.

(Cartago Province, Turrialba; www.guayabolodge.co.cr)

71. Have a Sky Diving Adventure in Quepos

If you fancy yourself as something of an adventurer, lying on the beach all day probably isn't going to cut it for you, but fear not because there are plenty of exciting adventures for thrill seekers in Costa Rica, and sky diving might just be the most adventurous of them all. Quepos is a small but busy town that's the centre of many adventure activities, and we think it's a great place for sky diving. You'll get an incredible view of Manuel Antonio Park as you freefall through the air.

72. Get to Grips With Costa Rican Beer in San Jose

Virtually every day in Costa Rica is baking hot, and what better way is there to cool down than with an ice cold beer? While Costa Rica might not be super famous for its beers, there is a growing artisanal beer culture that is well worth exploring, and Costa Rica Craft Brewing in San Jose is the very best place for exactly that. The folks here would be very happy to take you on a brewery tour, and to share some of the good stuff with you.

(San José Province, Brasil; http://beer.cr)

73. Celebrate the Dia de los Boyeros

Dia de los Boyeros, which can be translated as the Day of the Oxcart Drivers, is one of the most unique celebrations on the Costa Rican calendar. It's on the second Sunday of March in the town of Escazu that the residents celebrate the local agricultural heritage of the region. The main celebration on this day is a huge parade that starts from outside the main church of the town and goes all the way up into a small mountain town. Each year, there's more than 100 colourfully painted oxcarts that take part in the parade.

74. Hit a Few Golf Balls at Hacienda Pinilla

If you love nothing more than to visit your local golf club and hit a few balls on the weekend, we think that you'll be very impressed with the golf courses across Costa Rica. For our money, the very best of them all has to be Hacienda Pinilla in Santa Cruz. This 18 golf course is certainly a challenge because of the hilly terrain, but we think that the biggest distraction of all might be being distracted by the sight of the ocean.

(Santa Cruz, Tamarindo, 5150; www.haciendapinilla.com)

75. Start Your Day With an Espresso From Cafeoteca

If you are the kind of person who cannot function without a morning cup of coffee, you're in luck because

Costa Rica is a nation of coffee lovers. Still, when you're in a city for the first time, it can be difficult to know where's the best place to go for a caffeine hit. Luckily, you have us to direct you towards Cafeoteca in San Jose. With just ten seats, you might have to take your coffee to go, but whether you stay or go, it's the best coffee in town.

(http://kalu.co.cr/cafeoteca)

76. Spot Nesting Green Turtles at Parque Nacional Tortuguero

Turtles are some of the most beautifully majestic creatures on this planet, and the ultimate destination for turtle spotting in Costa Rica is the Parque Nacional Tortuguero, a protected wilderness area where many turtles come to nest. If you want to see something really spectacular, be sure to time your trip with the nesting and hatching season of the turtles, which takes place between April and November. At this time, you might just see newly hatched turtles racing into the sea.

(Limón Province, Pococi;
www.tortugueroinfo.com/spa/info_tortuguero.htm)

77. Have a Diving Adventure off the Catalina Islands

Costa Rica has stunning coastline on both sides, and this means that there is ample opportunity to explore the incredible waters of the Pacific and the Caribbean. If you are feeling adventurous, one of the very best things you can do is go diving and experience the marine life right before your very eyes. For our money, the best place for a spot of diving is the Catalina Islands. In this area, you can see giant mantas, sharks, eels, sea turtles, and beautiful schools of tropical fish.

78. Drink a Granizado While Topping Up Your Tan

When you are lying on a Costa Rican beach and you need something to cool your body temperature down, a granizado is f'sure the way to go. A granizado is essentially the Costa Rican version of a snow cone, except it's better than any snow cone you've ever put in your mouth before. This is essentially a huge cup of shaved ice that is topped with powdered milk, vanilla ice, and condensed milk. You'll be back for seconds, we can guarantee it.

79. Go White Water Rafting on the Reventazon River

The Reventazon River in Costa Rica is 145 km long and flows into the Caribbean sea. It's very important for two reasons. Number one, it generates a lot of power, and secondly it's important for tourism because it's the most popular spot for white water rafting in the country. Parts of the river have Class II and Class II rapids, which means you might just be in for a bumpy ride, particularly if you choose to visit in the rainy season. There's also stunning wildlife all along the river.

80. Have an Artsy Day at the Museum of Costa Rican Art

Arts lovers are sure to have a magical time in Costa Rica, and one of the must-visit places in the country's arts map is the Museum of Costa Rican Art in San Jose. The museum has a staggering collection of 6000 art works, and everything in the museum has been crafted by a Costa Rican, making this the largest collection of local art in the country. Our favourite part of the museum is the sculpture garden in the back, where it's lovely to pass a peaceful hour.

(Calle 15, San José, 133391-1000; www.madc.cr)

81. Try Trout Fishing on the Rio Savegre

If you are the kind of person that likes to spend weekends with a fishing rod in your hand in the quietude of nature, you'll have ample opportunity to enjoy a fishing adventure in Costa Rica. And if it's river fishing that really gets you going, we can highly recommend putting your fishing rod into the wild waters of the Savegre River. The river is full of rainbow trout, so there's definitely an opportunity to get a good catch, and maybe even catch something for your supper later on that evening.

82. Sip on a Fiery Chiliguaro Cocktail

When you are on holiday, it is the one time of the year when you can totally treat yourself without having to consider the consequences at all. And that means that you'll be wanting to indulge in more than a cocktail or two. There are plenty of delicious cocktails to be enjoyed at beach shacks all over the country, but we are pretty fond of the Chiliguaro, which is not a drink for the faint hearted. The key ingredient is cacique guaro, which is a sugar cane liqueur, and this is combined with tomato juice, lemon juice, and tobacco. It takes hair of the dog to a whole new level.

83. Help Clean a Beach on International Beach Clean-Up Day

Costa Rica has an absolutely stunning assortment of beaches, but those beaches can only remain paradise spots of sea and sand if they are looked after correctly. And that's why International Beach Clean-Up Day is so important. As the name would suggest, this day is celebrated internationally, but there is a very strong focus on Costa Rica because of its beautiful beach towns and villages. The day lands in September each year, so why not offer your support and help to clean up a Costa Rican beach?

84. Watch a Movie at Cine Magaly

Of course, Costa Rica is a country that is filled with plenty to see and do, but travelling can be exhausting, and there might be afternoons when you all you want to do is chill out with a great movie. When that afternoon comes, you need to know about the Cine Magaly. This is an independent cinema so going there feels more special than one of the blockbuster complexes in the city, and they often show arthouse movies in English.

(Calle 23, San José; https://cinemagaly.com)

85. Explore the Caves in Barra Honda

Costa Rica is not a country that is especially well known for its caves, but if you cannot resist a cave, the place to go is the Barra Honda National Park. Barra Honda is a huge hill that people used to believe was a volcano until the cave system was discovered there in the 1960s. Of all the 42 caves, only one of these, La Cuevita, is open to the public, and you'll need to take a local guide if you want to explore inside. The only way to get inside is to rappel down, so it's quite the adventure.

86. Feel the Country's Creative Pulse at eNe

If you have yet to buy any souvenirs from your trip to Costa Rica, trust us when we say that a little boutique design shop called eNe is all that you need. Located in the capital, San Jose, this is the place to grab the cutest design pieces from local artisan pieces. You'll be able to get your hands on all manner of great stuff, so whether you want some prints from an up and coming photographer or you'd like to take some hand crafted jewellery back with you, you'll find it at eNE.

(Entre Av 7 y Calle 11A, San José)

87. Make New Friends at Banana Beach on Playa Santa Teresa

Santa Teresa is a tiny beach village. It's exactly the kind of place that people take photos of to make their friends at home super jealous, and you could be one of those people. But even though it's a beach village, it comes to life at night, and the most popular beach bar is called Banana Beach. And if you are more of a day drinker, you can also relax on one of their day beds with a cocktail in hand while making friends with other travellers.

(Villa Bonita Dr, Puntarenas Province; https://bananabeachcr.com)

88. Wave a Rainbow Flag for Gay Pride in San Jose

Latin America has historically been one of the most progressive places in the world for LGBT rights in the world, and while Costa Rica does recognise same sex relationships, gay marriage is still not allowed. To celebrate how far the country has come but also to push for further equalities, there is a Gay Pride event in San Jose every year. This celebration happens at the end of June each year, and culminates with a colourful parade that takes over the whole downtown area.

89. Go Cigar Shopping at Rincon del Habano

While it's true that cigars are certainly more famous in Cuba than they are in Costa Rica, if you are partial to a puff on a high quality cigar, the place to get yours is the Rincon del Habano in San Jose. In this shop, you can find an international array of cigars with an emphasis placed on the wares of Central America. You will even be able to find beautiful cigars that have been crafted on home soil in Costa Rica.

90. See Wild Dolphins at Drake Bay

With so much coastline, Costa Rica is one of the best places to visit in the world if you happen to be interested in marine life, and the isolated spot of Drake Bay is actually considered one of the best places for dolphin and whale watching in the whole world. There are a few tour companies in the area that can take you out on the open waters so you can spot this majestic creatures, and you'll even have the opportunity to do some snorkelling in the ocean.

91. Eat a Pati at a Local Bar

When you think of Costa Rican food, what immediately springs to mind? There actually isn't that much famous grub from Costa Rica that is known around the world, but that is not to say that you can't find all kinds of deliciousness, and one of our favourite bar food and street snacks is called a pati. These are essentially empanadas that are filled with spiced meats. Simple but delicious.

92. Discover More Than 100 Birds at Zoo Ave

Set in the middle of the countryside, Zoo Ave is the perfect place to get away from it all while becoming better acquainted with the animals of Costa Rica. While this place is officially a zoo, it's actually more like a rescue centre, and you can find over 100 species of native birds here. And if birds don't quite do it for you, it's also possible to get up close and personal with wild cats, reptiles, Costa Rican monkeys, as well as creepy crawlies from the jungle.

(Hacia el B° San José., Provincia de Alajuela; http://rescateanimalzooave.org)

93. Attempt Not to Get Sloshed on Tumba Calzones

One of the most original drinks that we have tasted in Costa Rica is called a Tumba Calzon, and this drink is made exclusively in the Escazu brewery. The name of this drink literally translates as "panty remover" and after a few of these heady drinks, you might understand why. This drink is actually a kind of beer, but it tastes way stronger, without being unpleasant. The taste resembles hibiscus, but when it goes down it packs a punch like moonshine.

94. Buy Woodcraft Made From Coffee Roots at Cachi Dam

If you want to get away from it all, the tiny town of Cachi is a great choice. This place is most famous for its dam, and it's surrounded by natural beauty with forests and coffee plantations. But another reason that people visit Cachi is for its very unique woodcraft. What makes it so unique is that all the objects are made from the tough roots of the coffee plant. It could be a place to take something special back home with you.

95. See a Phenomenal Collection of Orchids at Lankester Gardens

Costa Rica has no shortage of stunning natural beauty and landscapes, but if its colourful flowers that really get you going, we can highly recommend a trip to the Lankester Gardens. These botanical gardens have lots of stunning plants and flowers, but it's really the orchids that steal the show, and as these flowers are surprisingly difficult to spot in the wild, this is definitely the place to look at them. This garden has more than 3000 species in all.

96. Visit the Stunning Iglesia de San Rafael

While Costa Rica might be more famed for its natural beautiful than its buildings, there are a handful of stunning churches around the country that are definitely worth visiting. The Iglesia de San Rafael, which is located in the small, picturesque town of Zarcero has to be one of the most distinctive churches you will ever see. Instead of using conventional white or stone colours, this church is created in pink and blue, so it really stands out against the natural landscapes.

97. Snack on Chalupas at the Bar

You might have tried a tostada before, but have you tried a chalupa? Well, chances are you actually have because chalupa is actually just the Costa Rican name for a Mexican tostada. These are great snacks, and you can often find them being sold very cheaply on the streets and as bar snacks. Chalupas in Costa Rica are typically loaded with black beans and salsa, so vegetarians have the option to enjoy these as well.

98. Take a Traditional Boruca Mask Home With You

If you really want to understand Costa Rica, you have to take the time to stray away from the beach, and understand some of the indigenous traditions of the Boruca indigenous people. One of the most important aspects of this culture is the Boruca mask. These masks are often worn for important festivals, and they are separated into two categories: devils and animals. Galeria Nemu in San Jose is a good place to purchase these.

99. Treat Yourself to a Decadent Meal at Café de Los Deseos

Costa Rica is certainly not the cheapest country in all of Central America, but this doesn't mean that you should rough it all the time, and sometimes it's important to indulge. Trust us when we say that there is no better place for an indulgent meal you'll never forget than at Café de Los Deseos in San Jose. This is an artsy colourful, young place with a realty great menu. The handmade tortillas made with local cheese are particularly great.

(Calle 15, Provincia de San José)

100. Snack on Chicharrones on the Street

In any country, some of the best food that you will ever find is sold by street vendors on the street, and this is no different in Costa Rica. One of our favourite nibbles to tuck into while walking the streets in chicharron, or pork rinds. Each portion of these has a huge amount of cholesterol, so it might not be something to eat every day, but while you're on holiday you can throw caution to the wind! These are also popular snacks in late night bars.

101. Party on the Beach at The Lazy Mon

If you love to party but you are not so much of a city person, fear not because the parties in Costa Rica are certainly not confined to San Jose. In fact, you can find parties in loads of the beach towns on both sides of the country's coastline. For us, one of the best places for a beach party is at The Lazy Mon, a beach bar in Puerto Viejo. The sunset happy hour cannot be beaten, and there is often live music throughout the night.

(Stanford's on the Beach, 70403, Provincia de Limón; www.thelazymon.com)

Before You Go…

Thanks for reading **101 Coolest Things to Do in Costa Rica.** We hope that it makes your trip a memorable one!

Keep your eyes peeled on **www.101coolestthings.com**, and have a wonderful time in Costa Rica.

Team 101 Coolest Things

20133989R00039

Printed in Poland
by Amazon Fulfillment
Poland Sp. z o.o., Wrocław